SEE INSIDE

AN ANCIENT GREEK TOWN

SERIES EDITOR: R.J. UNSTEAD

Kingfisher Books

Series Editor
R. J. Unstead

Author
Jonathan Rutland

Illustrators
Bill Stallion, Linden Artists,
Tudor Art

Kingfisher Books, Grisewood & Dempsey Ltd,
Elsley House, 24–30 Great Titchfield Street,
London W1P 7AD

First published in paperback in 1986 by Kingfisher
Books. Originally published in hardcover in 1979.

10 9 8 7 6 5 4 3 2

BRITISH LIBRARY CATALOGUING IN PUBLICATION DATA
Rutland, Jonathan
    See inside an ancient Greek town. – 2nd ed.
    (See inside).
    1. City and town life – Greece – History –
    Juvenile literature   2. Greece – Social life
    and customs – Juvenile literature
    I. Title
    938'.009'732   DF78

ISBN 0 86272 204 7

Printed in Hong Kong

CONTENTS

The Town	4
The Agora	6
Temple and Gods	8
Gymnasium and Stadium	10
At Home	12
Government and Defence	14
At Work	16
Daily Life in the Town	18
The Theatre	20
The Acropolis at Athens	22
Important Happenings	26
The Gods and Goddesses of Greece	28
Glossary of Terms	29
Index	31

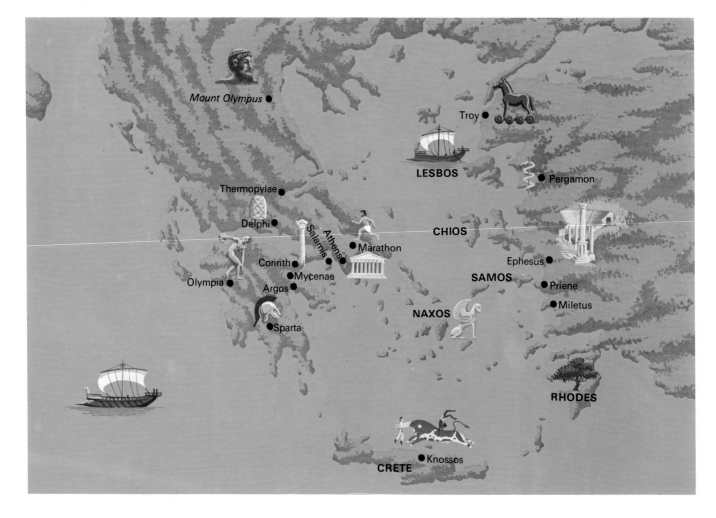

Ancient Greece

Greece is a small rocky country jutting out into the Mediterranean Sea. A legend tells how when God made the world he had a heap of stones left over. He threw them into the sea and they became Greece.

Nearly 4000 years ago people called the Minoans lived on the Greek island of Crete. They had splendid palaces, and they played a strange 'bull game' in which acrobats leaped up at a charging bull, grasped its horns, and somersaulted into the air. The Minoan cities were destroyed by a gigantic volcanic explosion on a nearby island.

Between about 1600 BC and 1200 BC, the Mycenaean civilization, so-called from its main town Mycenae, grew up on the Greek mainland. Raiders from the north, called Dorians, destroyed the Mycenaean civilization. You can read about some of the great kings and heroes of this time in the Iliad and the Odyssey – two books by the Greek writer Homer.

City states

The mountains of Greece divide the land into a lot of small areas, each one cut off from its neighbours. Each area now became a sort of miniature country. The people built a fort so that they could defend themselves, and for extra safety they built their homes around the fort. At first these tiny city states were usually ruled by a king, a tyrant, or by a small group of men. But in time citizens in many of the towns decided that they all wanted to share the running of their state. This is called democracy. The growth of these democratic city states took place between about 1100 BC and 500 BC. The hundred years which followed are called the age of Classical Greece. In this book we shall be looking at a typical city state of that time and observing the everyday lives of the people who lived there.

Above: This is the ruined Council Hall at Priene, a typical Greek town. Notice the hill behind, on which the fort was built to defend the town.

Below: This Athenian vase shows women slaves teasing out wool on the left, and spinning it on the right. In the centre two slaves are folding a blanket made from the wool.

The Town

The first stage in forming a city state was to build the fort. It was called the *acropolis*, and was always placed on top of a hill because this was the easiest spot to defend. In the town shown on these pages, the acropolis is off the top of the picture. After a while, people from the farms and villages around built houses near the acropolis, and slowly the town grew. The earlier towns of the Minoans and Mycenaeans were built around the ruler's palace, and were not planned.

The town wall goes up the hill round the back of the acropolis, sited on the top of it, and comes out on the other side of the hill. Notice that because the town is built on a steep hill, the 'streets' running up and down the hill are mostly flights of steps.

Greeks of the Classical era, however, were keen town planners. They laid the streets out in rows which crossed each other neatly at right angles. In this town there are broad main streets running across the picture. Houses and other buildings are arranged in the 'blocks' between the streets. Finally the people built a wall to keep out raiders. This went right around the town and the acropolis.

In the centre of the town stands the *agora* (1), the market place where people could chat, discuss the running of their city state, do their shopping and so on. Other important public buildings are grouped around the agora. They include temples to various gods (2), the council hall or *bouleuterion* (3) and the theatre (4). The large buildings at the edge of the town are the gymnasium (5) and stadium (6).

The Agora

The agora is the open space in the centre of the picture. It was the town's market place and meeting place. The word agora at first meant a meeting or assembly, and this was really its most important purpose. It was there that the citizens came to discuss the running of their city state. The agora was the parliament or centre of government (see pages 14–15). So on days when the Assembly met, all the citizens would be there, and the agora would be even more crowded than usual.

Early in the morning it began to fill up with people from the town and the surrounding villages. Some brought goods to sell – anything from fish, meat, vegetables, cheese, wine, pottery, bronze ware and textiles, to goats, sheep and slaves. These tradesmen might set up stalls in the open space of the agora, or they might have shops in the buildings around it. They shouted out their wares to attract customers, and they haggled about prices. The scene must have been bustling, colourful and noisy, very like a busy street market today.

Other people coming to the agora included public officials who saw that nobody broke the law, checked that traders were not charging too much, and who inspected their scales, balances and measures.

Then there were people just out for a stroll and a chat, and others coming to look at public notices (for example, every citizen had to take his turn in military service, and from time to time a new list was put up about this). There might also be acrobats, who earned a living by travelling from town to town giving displays in the agora. And there would often be teachers, who would sit in a quiet corner and gather students around them. One group of Greek thinkers or philosophers got their name from the fact that they always taught in the colonnades around the agora. These roofed colonnades were called *stoas*, and the group of thinkers were known as Stoics.

In some agoras the surrounding buildings were just stoas. But usually, as here, rooms were built behind the stoas. These were used as offices for merchants, bankers, magistrates and so on, and of course as shops.

6

There were usually several important buildings around the agora apart from the shops, offices and colonnades. The larger of the two buildings on the left is a temple; the smaller one is a fountain house. In ancient Greek towns there was no piped water supply to the houses. A few people had a private well, but everyone else came to the fountain house for their water. The building at the top right hand corner is the Bouleuterion, or Council House.

The temple, the large building on the right, was built as a home for the god or spirit. The artist has cut away the picture so that you can see inside the cella (the name for the inner part). You can also see how the temple was built, with the roof resting on the main walls as well as on rows of columns inside and outside the walls. In the cella there is a statue of the god, and a small table where pilgrims placed gifts. The pilgrims entered the walled temple grounds (temenos) through the gateway (propylaeum) below, took their offering into the temple, and then came out to worship at the large outdoor altar (below left). Beside the gateway you can see an animal being prepared for sacrifice.

Temple and Gods

Most people who believe in God today think that there is just one god. But the Greeks believed in many gods. Each town, stream, grove of trees and lonely place had its special god. There were gods of love, hunting and war; gods with power over the harvest, fire, wine and sea. Before starting any venture or task, men prayed to whichever god looked after that task. If it was something really important, such as a long voyage, a war, or the harvest, they sacrificed (killed) an animal as an offering (a sort of gift) to the gods. When things went wrong, they believed it was because the gods were angry, and they prayed and offered sacrifices to try to calm the gods' mighty anger.

Because there were so many gods, there were many temples and shrines. In some towns the old fort or acropolis became a holy place, with several temples, including one to the god or goddess who looked after the town. Once a year the people held a festival to their town's god, with processions, sacrifices, feasting and games. (See also page 28).

Below: The most important gods of the classical era were called the Olympians, after their home on Mount Olympus. Here we can see five Olympian gods: Zeus, who was king of the gods and of men; his son Apollo who was god of the sun, Poseidon – god of the sea and earthquakes, Aphrodite – goddess of love, and Demeter – goddess of crops.

9

The dromos, above, was attached to the gymnasium, and was a practice area. Actual races and other public contests took place at the stadium. The photograph below shows the stadium at Delphi. The stadium was usually in a valley, with rows of stone seats sloping up the hill at either side and at one end. At the other end was a fine gateway. The race track was one 'stade' long (around 200 metres or 220 yards). There were races of one stade (the dromos or stadion), two (the diaulos), four (the hippios), and long-distance events of 24 stades.

Gymnasium and Stadium

The gymnasium and stadium were the town's sports centre and race track. The Greeks thought a healthy body was as important as good schooling and work; almost all citizens and their boys went to the gymnasium every day for exercise and training. The main gymnasium is on the facing page. The open space in the middle is the *palaestra*. This was at first just a wrestling ground, but later on it was also used for practising sports such as throwing the discus, boxing, the long jump, and so on. Philosophers came here too, to discuss their ideas with the young and intelligent athletes.

In wrestling, no holds were barred, the object being to throw your opponent to the ground. Boxing was rougher than it is today, and a contest called the *pankration* was rougher still. This combined boxing, wrestling and kicking. The fight went on until one man gave in. He showed this by raising his first finger if he was still able to!

The *dromos* (above) was mainly a practice race track, but it was also used for training in other sports – for example boxing, wrestling and javelin throwing.

The athletes wore no clothes. They were proud of their muscular and healthy bodies.

THE OLYMPIC GAMES

The Olympic Games took place every four years at Olympia in northern Greece. They are the origin of our Olympic Games today. The most important contest was the pentathlon in which each contestant took part in five sports. There were discus and javelin throwing contests, long jumps, wrestling, chariot racing, and running races. The Marathon race was not part of the Olympics.

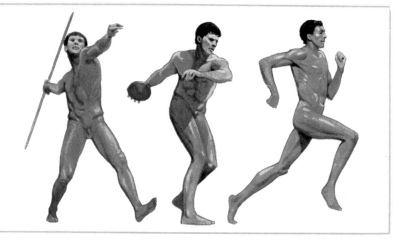

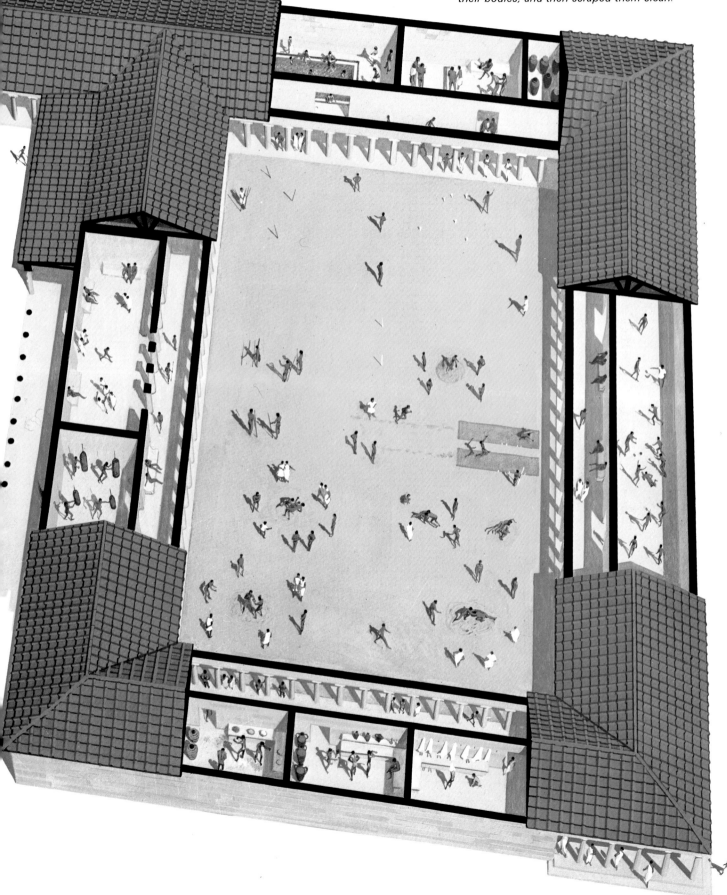

Around the central palaestra are changing rooms and practice rooms. There are also baths, a dust room (athletes covered their bodies with powder) and an anointing room. After exercise (and sometimes before) they oiled their bodies, and then scraped them clean.

This pottery statue shows a woman grilling meat over the kitchen fire. In fact, people rarely ate meat except at festivals. Fish was more usual. Breakfast and lunch were snacks – bread, cheese, fruit and wine. The main meal in the evening usually consisted of a first course of fish and vegetables, followed by fruit, and cakes made mainly from flour and honey. The food was served on pottery or metal plates, and eaten with a spoon and knife.

Most town houses were built on a stone base, although some had plain earth floors. The walls were made of mud bricks, and the upper floor and roof were held up by wooden beams. The mud bricks were not baked. They were very soft, and so were easily cut through by burglars – who were known as toichorychoi, 'wall diggers'.

At Home

A family house in town was built around an open courtyard. In the middle is a shrine to the household god, and underneath it there was sometimes a tank to collect and store rainwater. In front is a porter's small lodge. Most of the rooms looked inwards to the courtyard, and not out on to the street, which was noisy and smelly. Drains ran into an open gutter in the street. In the house in this picture, one of the front rooms is a storeroom, and another a pottery shop. The family live at the back. Upstairs at the back on the left are the women's living room and work room (where you can see them weaving).

Downstairs you can see the kitchen. There the women prepare and cook the food, and grind grain into flour. Smoke from the open fire escapes through a hole in the roof. Next door is the bathroom. In winter living rooms could be heated with charcoal fires burning in open hearths. To the left of the kitchen is the *andron*, the main room in the house. This is the men's dining and entertaining room. The men's quarters were more roomy than the women's, and often better decorated, with mosaic floors and painted walls.

A wooden staircase goes from the courtyard to a covered landing or gallery leading all the way round the first floor. From it doors open into the upstairs rooms. These were bedrooms, and quarters for the family's slaves. This house has a pitched and tiled roof, but many homes had flat roofs. These provided a pleasant place to sit on a warm evening.

Government and Defence

Above: A hoplite, or foot soldier. Armed with shield and spear, hoplites were the most important soldiers. A battle usually consisted of a line of hoplites marching up to the enemy lines, then trying to hack its way through.

Below: The woman in this sculpture represents Democracy. She is placing a crown on a man, who represents the citizens of Athens.

Today the people of most countries have a small share in the running of their nation. They choose the members of parliament who actually decide things. But there are far too many people for everyone to meet and discuss government. The democracy of an ancient Greek city state was quite different. The state was small, and all citizens could take part in the Assembly (women and slaves were not citizens, so they could not join in).

Citizens thought that government was one of the most important things in their life, so they went to the Assembly even though they were not paid to go. The Assembly met at the agora about once a month, and more often if necessary. Anyone could stand up and speak – if the others would listen to him. The citizens of Greek city states were the first people to use democratic government. Most of them worked to earn a living – farming, making goods to sell, and so on. They could only leave their work to go to the Assembly because they had slaves to carry on the work.

The Council

In addition to the Assembly, the town had a council. This was much smaller. It met in the Council House (see page 7). Its members were chosen by lot (this is like picking names out of a hat), and they were paid for their work. The Council's job was to help the Assembly. For example, if the Assembly had a lot of things to discuss, the Council would make a list of topics. Within the Council was a still smaller group, called the *prytany*, which met every day. Its task was to see that the things decided by the Assembly were carried out.

One of the jobs of any government is to see that the state is safe from enemies. The city states had no full time army, all citizens were part-time soldiers. If the city wanted to start a war, or had to defend itself, the citizens who were on 'soldier duty' at the time had to drop everything and fight. Most wars only lasted a few weeks, so the survivors were soon back at work.

Athens and Sparta were the largest city states or *poleis* and came to control many other city states. There was great rivalry between Athens and Sparta so they were often at war with each other. But it was not only the large city states that fought, small villages would attack each other ferociously to decide border disputes and other disagreements which were often very trivial. The town or village that lost the battle was destroyed, the men executed and the women and children sold into slavery.

Judges, like council members, were chosen by lot. As today, their task was to listen to both sides in a quarrel, and decide who was right. There were no lawyers. The citizens spoke for themselves. But they could pay someone to help them decide what to say to the judge.

DISMISSED IN DISGRACE

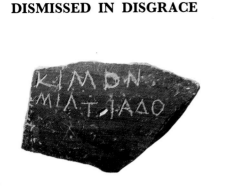

In some cities a citizen could be banished (forced to leave) for 10 years. There was no trial. This was called ostracism. If the Assembly decided it wanted to vote on ostracism, every citizen wrote down the name of the person he wanted ostracized. If enough people wrote the same man's name, he was banished from the state. People wrote the names on *ostraka*, fragments of stone like the one above.

Some Greek battles were fought at sea. They had special war galleys called triremes. These were rowed by several tiers of oarsmen, and had a ram at the bow for battering enemy ships. The Greek merchant ships are often called 'round ships'. They were broader and slower, and were propelled by sails.

This bust is of Pericles, one of the most famous statesmen of ancient Greece. He lived in Athens; and was such a good speaker at the Assembly that he became almost like a prime minister. He wanted to make Athens more powerful and more beautiful. Through his work, the buildings of the Acropolis were erected.

15

a blacksmith

Left: A pot showing a
potter at work.

QUARRYING

Most houses were built of mud
bricks, but large public buildings
were made of stone. The builder
told the quarryman what size blocks
he needed. At the quarry slaves cut
grooves in the rock, and hammered
wedges of wood into them. Then
they soaked the wedges in water.
This made the wood swell – which
in turn broke off the block. The
stones were roughly squared off
before being taken to the building
site. There, stone masons cut and
chipped the blocks into exactly the
right sizes and shapes. Often they
carved beautiful designs on them
too; for this they used marble.

*Blocks of building stone from the quarry were
taken down the mountain on rollers or
wooden sleds. Then they could be hauled
along by oxen, as you can see in the large
picture. The smaller picture shows how stones
were taken across water. They were hung
from a beam fixed between two boats (a
clever idea, as things weigh much less than
normal when in water). In the large picture you
can see how the wooden scaffolding was used,
and how blocks were lifted into position by
men winding in a rope which ran up over a
pulley and down to the block (knobs were left
on the blocks to fix the rope to). The stones
were not cemented, but were sometimes fixed
together with metal clamps or pins.*

At Work

Almost all citizens earned a living from some kind of work.
Most had small workshops, and a few slaves to do the hard work.
They sold their goods themselves. There were some traders who
bought goods from the maker or farmer, and sold them at a
higher price, but these men were not liked.

The Greek citizen preferred being his own boss. But there
were always some who worked for others, and some who were
out of work. They gathered in the agora early in the morning,
hoping to find someone who would hire them for the day.

The picture above on the left shows the work of a potter.
Next is a blacksmith at work. He made anything from braziers
and ploughs to weapons. The third picture shows a shoemaker
cutting out leather, and the fourth a fishmonger – who was
often also the fisherman. The last picture is of a doctor. Much
of his work was based on the studies of the famous Greek
physician Hippocrates. Instead of using magic, Hippocrates
tried to find out why people became ill, and how to cure them.
Dispensers (like today's chemists) sold remedies made from
roots, herbs and other plants.

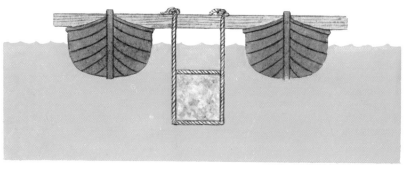

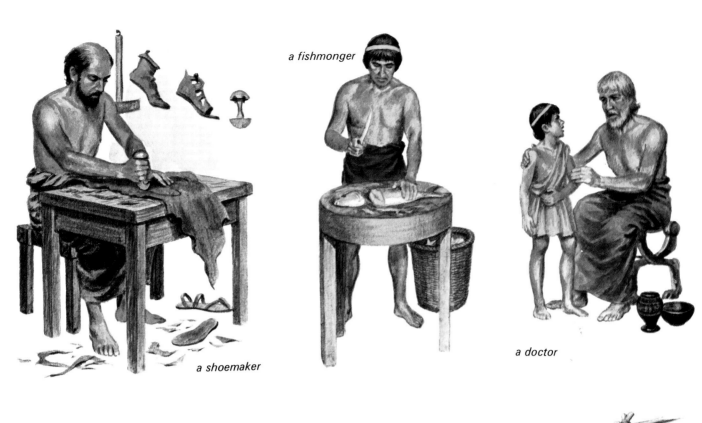

a fishmonger

a shoemaker

a doctor

In the classroom. Boys were taken to school each morning by a slave known as the paidagogos (our word pedagogue, teacher, comes from this ancient Greek word). As you can see there were no desks. Their 'pen' had one sharp end, for writing on their wax tablets, and a rounded end for rubbing out. As well as reading, writing and counting (with an abacus), boys learned music and poetry, and reciting poetry while playing the lyre. They also studied dancing. Boys left school at the age of 15.

The picture on the left shows slaves at work. Most slaves were captured in war. They were sold in the market. They worked as door-keepers, cooks, teachers, street cleaners and so on. House slaves were often treated as one of the family, but many others had a very rough life. If a slave could save enough money, he could buy his freedom. But he could not become a citizen.

The Greeks liked simple clothes which hung loosely, allowing plenty of freedom to move. The basic garment for both men and women (2 and 4) was the chiton *or tunic over which was worn an outer garment called a* himation. *This was made of wool, and could be wrapped around in many ways. The Greeks did not wear underclothes. The* peplos *(1 and 3) was held on by brooches at the shoulder, and worn with a belt.*

Rolling hoops was a popular pastime for boys. The hoops were made of iron, and some had jingling bells fixed to them.

GAMES AND PASTIMES

Hunting was a favourite pastime for men. There were foxes, wild boars, wolves and bears, and they were hunted with spears, axes, clubs and with dogs called Lakonian hounds. The children had toys made of wood, clay, leather and beeswax. They enjoyed ball games (one popular game was played pick-a-back), balancing games, and others like blind-man's-buff and tug-of-war. They played 'marbles' with walnuts.

Daily Life in the Town

The Greek playwright Aristophanes wrote: 'At the crack of dawn, when the cock crows, everybody awakes and sets off to work. They all dress in a hurry and set off while it is still dark'. He was writing about the male citizens and their male slaves, for women – both free ones and slaves – spent most of their time in the house. The mistress of the house set her slaves to work making bread, preparing other foods, and perhaps teaching them how to spin and weave. The mistress herself might do some weaving, and make the finished cloth into clothing by dyeing and ornamenting the material. There was no need to cut the fabric into sleeves or to sew it because the 'sheet' of woven material was simply draped over the body.

The mistress of the house managed the family's money and looked after her children. But in some ways she was treated like a slave. Her husband expected her to stay at home, not to argue, and to stay out of the way when he had guests. If there was shopping to be done, he did it, not her. Normally he went out at dawn, to work, to shop, to chat and discuss affairs with others at the agora, to exercise at the gymnasium, and perhaps even to go hunting. He did not return home until nightfall, when it was time for dinner.

All children stayed at home until they were six years old, unless their parents did not want them. In that case they took the child outside and left it to die. After their sixth birthday, boys were sent off to school. But there were no girls' schools. Girls might be taught by their mothers, or by slaves. They usually learned reading, writing, music and dancing. They were also taught how to cook and weave, and all the other things to do with running the home. Boys left school at 15. At 18, an Athenian boy became a citizen and promised to defend his country and obey the laws. He would spend a year training to be a soldier, and then, if his family were rich, instead of working he might enrol in a sports academy.

The Theatre

Before the era of classical Greece people used to gather around the circular patch of ground used for threshing wheat to watch songs and dances to the gods. By the classical era, the threshing floor had been replaced by huge outdoor theatres like the one in the picture.

A visit to the theatre was one of the most exciting and important events for the people of an ancient Greek town. It was really a religious festival, and it was one of the few public events attended by both men and women. Entry cost two obols (one third of a drachma), but anyone who could not afford this was allowed in free. Plays were put on about once a month, and the performance lasted all day – so the audience took food in with them. There were three serious full-length plays, with an interval between each, and the day ended with a light-hearted farce, so everyone went home happy.

The plays were about well known heroes, legends and myths, so everyone knew the basic story. But it was always exciting to see how the playwright told the story, and how the actors performed it. The audience showed their enjoyment by whistling, and stamping their feet. But if an actor made a mistake they shouted and booed, and sometimes even threw stones at him.

The main actors performed on the upper stage. Women were not allowed to act, so men acted female parts in the plays. Each actor played several characters, changing his costume and mask in the dressing-rooms behind the stage. The story was acted on the raised stage. The actors playing in the orchestra, at ground level, were the chorus. The dramatist used the chorus, who danced and sang as a group, to tell the audience what he thought about the incidents in the story.

Rows and rows of tiered stone seats rise up the hillside around the 'stage'. The seats were often cut out of the rock. Important people sat in more comfortable seats at the front. They included the judges who awarded prizes for the best plays. The stage is in two parts. First there is the round area of beaten earth in the middle, called the orchestra. *Behind this is a colonnaded building called the* proskenion. *The second stage is built on top of this, and is called the* logeion. *Behind this raised stage stands the* skene.

In such huge theatres, most of the audience are unable to see the actors' faces clearly. So they wear large masks. The face on the mask shows what sort of character he is.

Actors come on to the raised stage through doors in the skene. There are usually three, the middle one being the 'home' of the main character in the play, the side doors those of the less important characters. Actors in the orchestra enter from either side of the proskenion which is painted to provide 'scenery' for the plays. Some ancient Greek theatres have been restored, and are being used today for performances of famous plays by dramatists of classical Greece.

The Acropolis at Athens

Athens is the capital of Greece today and has been since ancient times the country's largest and most important city. The acropolis, shown in the picture above, was once a hill top fort. The town grew around the fort, and in time the acropolis was turned into a holy place with many fine temples. There was only one way up the rocky hillside to the acropolis, and only one entrance, through the Propylaeum (the entrance building).

The goddess, Athena, watched over Athens, and gave the city her name. The buildings of the acropolis were designed as a home for her. The largest and most important temple, the Parthenon, was her temple. In the middle of the acropolis you can see a statue of Athena.

The picture shows the Athens acropolis as it was in ancient times. Today, many of the buildings are in ruins, but the acropolis is still one of the world's most famous sights, and people from all over the world travel to Athens to see it. The Greek government is worried that their footsteps will wear away the stone paths and the floors of the buildings.

1. Temple of Athena
2. The Propylaeum (gateway)
3. Statue of Athena
4. The Parthenon
5. Great Altar of Athena
6. Sanctuary of Zeus
7. The Erectheion – it houses the oldest known image of Athena.
8. Administrative Offices

WEIGHTS, MEASURES AND MONEY

Until about 650 BC the people of Greece did not use money. All 'buying' and 'selling' had to be done by exchange, which could be very awkward and complicated. In the classical era the Greeks had two units of money, the obol, and the drachma (worth 6 obols). The usual coins were the half-obol, the obol, the drachma and the two- and four-drachma pieces. Most citizens earned around half a drachma a day.

Units of length were the finger and the foot. A finger equalled 19.3 mm ($\frac{3}{4}$ in). There were 16 fingers to a foot, and 24 fingers to an 'olympic cubit'. The unit of weight was the talent (25.8 kg, 57.0 lb) and that of liquids – and volume – the metretes (39.4 litres, 8.6 gal).

Greek numbers were represented by letters. I = 1, Π = 5, Δ = 10, H = 100, X = 1000, and M = 10,000. This made working sums as we do with neat columns for hundreds, tens and units, impossible. Most counting was therefore done with an abacus or counting frame.

GREEK THINKERS

This bust is of Plato, one of the most important of the Greek philosophers. He was the pupil of Socrates and the master of Aristotle, two other great philosophers.

The classical Greek era was a time when people thought a lot about the universe, about their lives, about why they did things, and so on. They enjoyed asking questions, and seeing if they could find answers. People like this are called philosophers – a word that in Greek means 'lovers of wisdom'. Today people still study the philosophers of ancient Greece such as Plato, Socrates and Aristotle. In a book called the Republic, Plato tried to work out the best way to run a country. He decided that states should be governed by 'philosopher kings'. Socrates asked questions like 'what is courage?' while Aristotle studied a huge range of subjects (in those days all knowledge was part of philosophy).

Overleaf: A vase decorated with a painted scene of a woman being dressed by a slave.

GREEK ALPHABET

A	α	alpha	a	I	ι	iota	i	P	ρ	rho	r
B	β	beta	b	K	κ	kappa	k	Σ	σ,s	sigma	s
Γ	γ	gamma	g	Λ	λ	lambda	l	T	τ	tau	t
Δ	δ	delta	d	M	μ	mu	m	Υ	υ	upsilon	u, y
E	ε	epsilon	e	N	ν	nu	n	Φ	φ	phi	ph
Z	ζ	zeta	z	Ξ	ξ	xi	x (ks)	X	χ	chi	kh, ch
H	η	eta	ē	O	o	omicron	o	Ψ	ψ	psi	ps
Θ	θ	theta	th	Π	π	pi	p	Ω	ω	omega	o

IMPORTANT HAPPENINGS

	Greece	Europe
BC 3000	*c*3000-1500 The Minoans flouish on the island of Crete. *c*2000-1700 Greek-speaking tribes arrive in Greece. *c*1600-1200 The Mycenaen civilization arises in the citadel-towns of Mycenae and Tiryns. *c*1500 The biggest explosion ever occurs when volcanoes erupt on the island of Thera. Huge waves engulf Crete. *c*1450 Cretan civilization destroyed.	*c*3000 New Stone Age in northern Europe. *c*1800-1400 Stonehenge built in Britain (2nd–3rd phase). *c*1500-1300 Bronze Age in northern Europe.
BC 1200	*c*1200 The end of the siege of Troy. After ten years, the Greeks led by Agamemnon capture Troy. *c*1200-800 Invaders from the north (in particular, the Dorians) start the collapse of the Mycenaean civilization. The Mycenaean kings speed it up by fighting among themselves. *c*850 Homer wrote the *Iliad* and the *Odyssey*. These poems tell the story of the siege of Troy, and of the Greek heroes' return to their homeland. 850-650 Rise of city states. 776 The first Olympic Games take place. Apollo worshipped at Delphi. 650-594 Some city states turn towards democracy. In 594 the Athenian statesman Solon draws up a new set of laws which encourage democracy.	*c*1100 Phoenician colonies in Spain. 900 Rise of Etruscans in Italy. 753 Traditional date of the founding of Rome. *c*700 Hallstatt culture—first use of iron. 600 Greeks found city of Massilia (Marseilles) in France. 510 Founding of the Roman Republic. Roman nobles drive out their Etruscan kings. 494 Plebeians (workers) of Rome rebel against nobles. They win some rights.
BC 508	508 Athenian democracy begins. 499-494 Greek colonists in Asia Minor revolt against Persian rule. The revolt fails and in: 490 The Persians attack Greece itself. They are defeated at Marathon, after which Pheidippides is supposed to have run the 40 kilometres (25 miles) from Marathon to Athens with news of the victory. 480-479 The Persians send another army against Greece, and win the Battle of Thermopylae, but are defeated in the sea-battle of Salamis and finally at Plataea. This opens an era of peace which enables the city states to develop. 460-429 Athens dominates the Aegean and enjoys its Golden Age under Pericles. 431 The Peloponnesian War between Athens and Sparta results in more than two decades of fighting on land and at sea. 404 Athens finally surrenders to Sparta. 362 Epaminondas of Thebes defeats Spartans. 338 Philip of Macedon invades Greece, end of Greek independence. 336 Philip is murdered and his son Alexander succeeds him and crushes Greek opposition. 334-327 Alexander the Great destroys Persian power and conquers an empire stretching from Egypt to north India.	*c*450 Celtic La Tène culture develops in central and northern Europe. 396-290 Rome conquers Etruscans and the Latin tribes; becomes master of Italy. 390 Gauls capture Rome, but withdraw.
BC 323	323 Alexander dies at Babylon aged 32. End of the Great Age of Greece.	

Near East	East Asia	
*c*3100 First writing in Mesopotamia. *c*3100 First Egyptian Dynasty. *c*2686-2181 Egypt's Old Kingdom. *c*2500 Akkadian Empire founded by Sargon in Sumeria. *c*2050-1786 Egypt's Middle Kingdom. *c*1800-1750 Hammurabi rules Babylon. **1567-1085** Egypt's New Kingdom—the XIX Dynasty (1320-1200) and the XX Dynasty (1200-1085).	*c*2500 Indus Valley civilization arises in India. *c*2000-1500 Legendary Hsia Dynasty in China. *c*1500 Indus Valley civilization falls to invaders. *c*1500-1027 Shang Dynasty in China; the Bronze Age; Anyang becomes capital.	**BC 3000**
*c*1380-1240 Hittite Empire at its height in Asia Minor. *c*1200 Sea Peoples raid Mediterranean coasts. Hebrews occupy Canaan. **1150** Greeks begin to colonize coast of Asia Minor. **1085-333** Egypt's late Dynastic Period. **973** Solomon becomes King of Israel.	*c*1027-771 Western Chou Dynasty in China.	**BC 1200**
705-682 Sennacherib, King of Assyria, establishes his capital at Nineveh (701). **670** Assyrians invade Egypt. **612** Medes and allies overthrow Assyrian Empire. **605-561** Nebuchadnezzar II rules as King of Babylon. **586** Nebuchadnezzar destroys Jerusalem. **539** Cyrus of Persia conquers Babylonia. **525** Persians invade Egypt. **486-465** King Xerxes rules the Persian Empire.	**722-256** Eastern Chou Dynasty: Golden Age of Chinese philosophy. **660** Jimmu Tenno, legendary first emperor of Japan accedes. **640** Birth of Chinese philosopher Lao-Tze. *c*600 Early cities near river Ganges in India; first ironworking in China. **563** Birth of the Buddha in Nepal, India. **551** Birth of Chinese philosopher Confucius. **533** Persians invade India, by now highly civilized, with towns, cities and extensive overseas trade. North-west India becomes a province of Persian Empire for 200 years. Introduction of Persian art and religion. **481-221** The Warring States period in China.	**BC 508**
360s Revolts in Persian Empire. **334-330** Alexander the Great defeats the Persians in Asia Minor and Syria, takes Jerusalem, founds Alexandria in Egypt, and, with the capture of Babylon, destroys the Persian Empire completely.	**327** Alexander the Great invades north India.	**BC 323**

THE GODS
AND GODDESSES OF GREECE

Bronze head of Apollo

Aphrodite
The goddess of love, beauty and fertility. She was born out of the sea-foam and carried on a shell to the island of Cythera, which, with Cyprus, was a main centre of her worship.

Apollo
The god of poetry, music, medicine, agriculture and prophecy, who was also identified with Helios, the sun god. The son of Zeus, he and his sister Artemis were born on the island of Delos. Apollo came to be venerated more than Zeus himself, because, as the god of prophecy, he drew worshippers and emissaries from all over Greece and neighbouring lands to his shrine at Delphi. There they would consult the oracle, a priestess whose mysterious replies to their questions were interpreted by temple priests.

Ares
The god of war, son of Zeus and Hera, and the lover of Aphrodite.

Artemis
Twin sister of Apollo, goddess of wild animals and childbirth, who was also the virgin huntress carrying bow and arrows.

Athena
Goddess of war and wisdom; patroness of arts and crafts and of the city of Athens. She sprang fully armed from the head of Zeus, after he had swallowed her mother, Metis. Frequently called Pallas Athena, she was worshipped in a number of roles, and her temple in Athens, the Parthenon, was the most celebrated in the Greek world.

Demeter
The goddess of Earth's fruits, especially corn. When her daughter Persephone (the seed corn) was carried off to the Underworld by Hades, Demeter's grief caused a famine on Earth until Zeus directed that Persephone should return to her mother above ground for two-thirds of the year. This explained the rising corn and the harvest.

Dionysus (also Bacchus)
The god of wine and intoxication who was honoured with songs, revels and merriment.

Hades or Pluto
The ruler of the gloomy Underworld, where the souls of the dead lived.

Hera
The goddess of marriage and childbirth. She was the wife of Zeus, and many stories tell of her constant nagging and jealousy.

Hermes
The messenger of the gods and protector of travellers who escorted the dead down to Hades. He wore a winged helmet and sandals.

Maenads
Female worshippers of Dionysus, who roamed about in a frantic drugged condition; hunting animals and devouring their raw flesh.

Moirae, the Fates
Usually portrayed as three old hags, the Fates were more powerful than the gods themselves, because they knew the past, the present and the future.

Muses
Nine goddesses who were the patrons of music, poetry, dance and literature.

Poseidon
The god of the sea, of earthquakes, streams and horses. He was the somewhat unruly brother of Zeus.

Zeus
King of the gods. He ruled the weather, and was usually shown armed with a thunderbolt. In some places he was also worshipped as the patron god of guests and the home.

Bronze head of Aphrodite

GLOSSARY OF TERMS

Acropolis A hill-top fort built on high ground to protect the city. The most famous acropolis in ancient Greece was that of Athens. 'Acro' means 'summit', and 'polis' means 'state'.

Agora The meeting place and market in the middle of a Greek town. It was a large open space surrounded by public buildings and temples.

Amphitheatre An oval or circular building with tiers of seats round a central open space.

Amphora A large clay pot, with two handles at the neck, used to store liquids such as wine or olive oil.

Archon One of the nine ruling magistrates of Athens. Archons were selected by lot to serve for one year. They supervised the law courts and public religious ceremonies.

Areopagus A hill in Athens, sacred to Ares, god of war. Later, the name was given to the council which met on the hill to judge cases of murder.

Assembly A meeting of all citizens to discuss the affairs of the city state and decide what should be done.

Boule The council, made up of 500 citizens, which governed Athens. The Boule prepared laws which were then passed on to the *Ecclesia* for the approval of the people. It also made sure that the laws were kept.

Bouleuterion The Council House.

Capital The carved top of a stone column. The three main types of Greek columns were the Doric, Ionic, and Corinthian orders.

Cella The inner part of a Greek temple in which the statue of the god stood. The entrance to the cella always faced to the east.

Chiton A Greek tunic of wool or linen worn by men and women. It was made of two lengths of material pinned or sewn together at the shoulders and gathered at the waist.

Citizen In Athens only people who could vote at the Assembly were called citizens.

Council A group of citizens whose job was to help the Assembly.

Crater (krater) A pottery bowl, in which the Greeks mixed water and wine.

Demes (demoi) All of Attica was divided into small parishes, called demes. A deme numbered between 600 and 1200 citizens. It sent representatives to the Boule and provided soldiers for the army. When the son of a citizen reached his eighteenth birthday, his name was entered on the voting roll of his deme. In this way he was officially made a citizen.

Democratia (Democracy) Literally, 'rule by the people'. In Athens, this meant that all citizens had an equal right to take part in government. Also, no law could be passed without the approval of the Ecclesia, to which every citizen over the age of 20 belonged.

Dromos A running track.

Ecclesia The assembly of the Athenian people. It met regularly on the Pnyx, a low hill to the west of the Acropolis. All citizens over the age of 20 were automatically members. Although the day-to-day running of Athens was left to the Boule, the final decision on any issue rested with the vote of the Ecclesia.

Frieze A band of stonework running along the sides of a Greek building, between the tops of the columns and the roofline. It was often decorated with sculptures.

Gerousia The council of the advisers to the two kings of Sparta. It was made up of 28 citizens over 60.

Helots Spartan slaves bound to the land. A fixed proportion of their produce went to feed the Spartan citizens. Helots had no legal rights, and were punished by death if they tried to escape.

Himation An outer garment worn for beauty or added warmth, usually made of wool.

The Greek year ran from midsummer to midsummer. These were the main festivals at Athens.

Greek month	English equivalent	Festival	Deity honoured
Skirophorion	June/July	Arrephoroi	Athena
		Dipoleia	Zeus
		Diisoteria	Zeus, Athena
Hekatombion	July/August	Panathenea	Athena
Roedromion	September/October	Mysteries of Demeter	
Pyanopsion	October/November	Chalkeia or	Athena and
		Feast of the smiths	Hephaestus
Maimakterion	November/December	Maimakteria	Zeus
Antihesteria	February/March	Lenaia	Dionysus
		Diasia	Zeus/Meilichios
Elaphebolion	March/April	Great Dionysia	Dionysus
Thargelion	May/June	Thargelia	Apollo, Artemis

There were many other minor festivals and celebrations throughout the year. In the bean-boiling feast of the Pyanepsia, children carried poles wound with wool from door to door, receiving gifts of fruit, bread, cakes, and jars of oil and honey. The Haephestia, in honour of Hephaestus the blacksmith of the gods, was celebrated at night with a torchlight race between teams of runners.

Hoplite The traditional foot soldier of a Greek city state. A citizen equipped himself at his own expense with bronze helmet, breastplate, leg-guards and shield. His short sword was of iron, and he carried a 3 metre (9 foot) long spear.

Logeion The raised stage at the theatre. It was the roof of the proskenion.

Megaron The main room in the simple, rectangular houses of early Greek chiefs. In the centre of the room was an open hearth, used for cooking and for religious ceremonies. The design became the basis of the Greek temple.

Mosaic A pattern or picture made up from hundreds of small pieces of differently coloured stone set in cement. In ancient Greece some floors were made in this way.

Olympians The name given to the main gods of classical Greece, after their home on Mount Olympus.

Oracles Places where the gods spoke to humans and replied to their questions. The best-known oracle was at Delphi, where Apollo 'spoke' through the mouth of a priestess, while she herself was in a trance. Greek cities regularly sent ambassadors to Delphi to ask the advice of Apollo.

Orchestra The round patch of beaten earth (the dancing floor) in the centre of the theatre.

Palaestra The wrestling ground or open area at the gymnasium. Later it was used for other sports.

Pankration A rough sport which combined wrestling, boxing and kicking.

Pentathlon The most important event in the Olympic Games. The athletes had to show their overall excellence by taking part in five different sports (penta means five). They were running, the long jump, throwing the discus and the javelin, and wrestling.

Peplos A woollen robe for women, made from a single length of cloth about 2 metres by 3 metres ($6\frac{1}{2}$ ft by 10 ft). It could be worn in several different ways, the simplest being to pin it at the shoulder leaving the right-hand side open. Every year, at the Panathenea (see page 29), a richly decorated peplos was carried in procession to the statue of Athena on the Acropolis. Then the peplos, which was made by the women of Athens, was presented to the goddess.

Peristyle A row of columns surrounding a courtyard or building.

Podium A raised platform, base or pedestal in a temple or round an amphitheatre.

Propylaeum The entrance building to the temple or other sacred area.

Proskenion The colonnade behind the orchestra at the theatre.

Prytany Small group of citizens made up from members of the council. It saw that everything decided by the council was carried out.

Pythia The priestess of Apollo at Delphi. At the time of its greatest fame there were three Pythias to deal with the stream of petitioners who had come to consult the oracle. During the ceremony, the Pythia, seated on a sacred bronze stool, entered a trance. After she had spoken the words which the god supposedly had put into her mouth, the temple priests turned her utterance into an answer which was usually so vague that it was unlikely ever to be proved wrong!

Sarcophagus A coffin or a container for a coffin made of stone or terracotta. The outside was often decorated with paintings or relief carvings and inscriptions.

Satyrs Spirits of woods and hills in human form with horses ears and tails. Associated with the wine god, Dionysus, they were forever engaged in wild revels and somewhat sinister merriment.

Skene The dressing rooms behind the raised stage at the theatre.

Stadium The sports ground where public contests were held.

Stadion A Greek running-track, oblong in shape, about 200 metres (218 yards) wide, with a turning-post at each end.

Stele A stone slab, often irregular in shape, which was set up as a marker. The best known are those put up over graves, which are often beautifully carved. They were also used as boundary stones.

Stoa A colonnade with a roof.

Temenos The walled temple area.

Trireme A war galley rowed by several tiers of oarsmen.

Tyrant A ruler in complete charge of a state. He was so powerful that he could do as he pleased irrespective of the people's wishes.

INDEX

A
abacus 23
acropolis 4, 5, 15, 22
agora 5, 6, 7, 14, 16, 19
alphabet 23
Aphrodite 9, 28
Apollo 9, 28
Ares 28
Aristophanes 19
Artemis 28
Assembly 6, 14, 15
Athena 22, 28
Athens 14, 22, 23
athletes 10

B
blacksmith 16
boats 15, 16
Bouleuterion 5, 7
building 4, 5, 12, 16

C
chorus 20
city states 3, 4, 5, 6, 14, 23
cloth 3, 12, 19
Council 3, 5, 7, 14
Crete 3, 23

D
dancing 19, 20
defence 3, 4, 5, 14, 15, 19, 23
Delphi 10
Demeter 9, 28
democracy 3, 14, 23
Dionysus 28
doctor 16, 17
Dorians 3

F
festivals 8
food 6, 12, 19
fort, 3, 4, 22

G
games 19
gods 8, 9, 12, 28
government 3, 5, 6, 14, 15, 22
gymnasium 5, 10, 19

H
Hades 28
Hera 28
Hermes 28
Hippocrates 16
Homer 3, 23
hoplite 14
houses 5, 12, 13
hunting 19

J
judges 6, 14, 20

L
legend of Greece 3

M
Maenads 28
Marathon 10, 23
market place 5, 6
measures 6, 23
military service 6, 19
Minoans 3, 4, 23
Moirae 28
money 18, 19, 20, 23
mosaics 12
mud bricks 12, 16
Muses 28
Mycenae 3, 4, 23

N
numerals 23

O
Olympic Games 10, 23
ostracism 15

P
Parthenon 22
pedagogue 18
Pericles 15, 23
Persians 23
Philip of Macedonia 23
philosophers 6, 10, 23
Plato 23
Pluto 28
Posiedon 9, 28
pottery 12, 16
Priene 3, 4, 5

Q
quarrying 16

S
sacrifices 8
school 18, 19
shoemaker 16, 17
slaves 6, 13, 14, 18, 19
soldiers 14, 19, 23
Solon 23
Sparta 14, 23
sport 10, 11, 19
stadium 5, 10

T
teachers 6, 18, 19
temples 7, 8, 22
theatre 20, 21
town-planning 5
Troy 23

W
water 7, 12, 16
   for building 16
weaving 12, 19

Z
Zeus 9, 28

PHOTOGRAPHIC ACKNOWLEDGEMENTS
The publishers wish to thank the following for supplying photographs for this book: Page 3 Metropolitan Museum of Art, New York *bottom*, Sonia Halliday *top*; 12 Ronald Sheridan; 14 Michael Holford; 15 British Museum *left*, Michael Holford *right*; 19 Ronald Sheridan; 22 Royal Museum, Ontario; 23 British Museum *left*, Ronald Sheridan *right*; 24–25 Michael Holford; 28 Michael Holford.

Picture research: Penny Warn.